DAILY WORD

PRAYER JOURNAL

A FORTY-DAY PROGRAM TO AWAKEN YOUR SOUL

Written and edited by Colleen Zuck,
Janie Wright, and Elaine Meyer

Berkley Books,
New York

CONTENTS

Section 3—Healing the Whole Person

Section 4—Living from the Sacred Soul

AWAKENING THE SACRED
SOUL THROUGH PRAYER

H ow do we pray and what should we feel as we pray? The answers are different for each of us, but one thing is common to us all: In prayer, we build a growing awareness of God—the spirit of God within us, within others, and within our world.

Why is this a forty-day prayer journal? While it is true that forty days has traditionally been seen by various world religions as a period of completion, it is also true that anything we do on a daily basis for a month or more tends to become a part of our lives and can affect us deeply. Thus, the few minutes we invest in prayer and journaling for forty days can result in an awakening of our sacred souls.

Awake spiritually, we are aware of the divine power that is within us. With this awareness at our soul level, we come face to face with our own spiritual identities as our humanness merges with our sacredness—the indwelling spirit of God—and we are transformed.

Describing the experience of prayer may be impossible, but we believe that this book will lead all people who are willing to let it happen into a *personal* communion with God. How can you experience such soul satisfaction? Think of yourself with such an incredible thirst that nothing but water can satisfy it. Imagine bringing a cup of fresh, clear water to your lips and tipping the cup. As the water starts to flow over your parched tongue and down your dry throat, every cell of your body awakens and is revived. There is a satisfaction that leaps forward and refreshes your *whole* being.

Now think about how the experience of prayer refreshes you. Your whole being awakens to the presence of God. And through this experience, you know the truth about yourself: You are a whole and sacred person—spirit, mind, and body. You realize that you have wisdom and strength you never before believed were possible. And as the drink of water satisfied the thirst of your body, your prayer time will satisfy the thirst of your soul.

The purpose of this book is to help you experience the indescribable, yet undeniable, experience of becoming one with God in prayer. Each day in this forty-day prayer journal, you are offered four types of spiritual enrichment: an inspirational quote, a universal prayer, a talking-to-God prayer, and a journal page. And along the way, short true-life stories will inspire you to move forward.

How to Use This Prayer Journal

1. Read each day's prayer. Take this book with you to a quiet place where you can linger undisturbed for ten minutes or so. Allow yourself to be comfortable and quiet. As you read the prayers written here, allow yourself to *feel* the words.

2. Experience prayer. Then, in the stillness, let the *experience* of prayer be your own—your own sacred communion with God.

3. Journal your thoughts. After your quiet time, write down the ideas that came to you during prayer. Each journal page offers a few suggestions to help get you started.

Follow these simple steps—prayer, quiet time, and journaling—for forty days and discover a new, healthier, more loving and peaceful *you* emerging.

4. Continue with prayer and journaling. Having awakened to your spiritual identity, you will never again forget who you are—not as you continue to pray and to capture your most inspired revelations on paper or in your mind.

Reserve some time each day for going over in your mind what you have experienced in prayer—what you thought, heard, and felt. Then every day, you will reawaken to your sacred soul.

During this time or at any other time, Silent Unity will pray with you—day or night. You can call the Silent Unity Prayer Ministry at (816) 969-2000. Or, if you prefer, write to Silent Unity at 1901 NW Blue Parkway, Unity Village, MO 64065-0001.

The Editors

Section 1

Discovering the Sacred

WORKS OF ART,
SIGNED BY GOD

BY FANNIE FLAGG, AUTHOR AND ACTRESS

My father's alcohol abuse not only took him away from me, it also took my mother, because all her attention was focused on him. We were both so focused on my father that we were cheated out of a normal mother-daughter relationship. I grew up a loner, afraid to care for anyone, terrified to trust in case my heart would be broken again as it was when I was a child.

But I felt even more alone when my parents died within three months of each other. In fact, I felt lost. I gave up my acting career and thought a lot about death and suicide. I was homesick, so I went back home to Alabama looking for . . . something, but I didn't know what. I began driving around to all the old places where I had lived as a child.

Then, on a cold, rainy November afternoon, I drove by the old family home. The beautiful two-story white-frame house where my grandmother, her brothers, and her sisters had been raised was nothing but an empty shell, much as I felt I was then. But on that dark afternoon, when the headlights of my car shone on the windows, for just a moment I saw the house the way it must have been years ago—all lit up and full of happy people. I stopped the car and cried for all the things that used to be. And out of that moment came the idea for a new novel, *Fried Green Tomatoes at the Whistle Stop Cafe*.

One of my characters, Mrs. Cleo Threadgoode, began to

teach me about God. I saw God through her eyes. The more I wrote, the more my characters helped me believe in God. They showed me how to love, how to be happy and appreciate things. They taught me about miracles . . . where to look for them and what they are.

I'm writing a new book, and the other day Aunt Elner, one of the characters, was telling a young man who said he had never had proof that God loved him to look at his own fingertips. She explained that God thought each one of us so special that He gave each and every one of us a completely different and unique set of fingerprints—as a sign that we are special.

She asked the young man, who was an artist, "Who else but the great Creator could create billions of different people and never repeat Himself?" The young artist was then able to see God as an artist and realize that each one of us is a work of art, signed by God.

For much of my life, I was scared and needed some sort of peace. It's taken a long time, but I'm making progress. All I have to do when I get stuck is look at my fingertips and remember that I'm a work of art, signed by God.

Day 1
♦
Breath of Life

"The search of all people is
for God. They may think they are
looking for other things, but
they must eventually admit that
it is God they seek."

—CHARLES FILLMORE

Prayer

By James Dillet Freeman

Prayer is a state of being, like snowfall
At night. As in the silence of yourself you pray,
All things particular, familiar, small
Or large, dissolve and slowly melt away.
Only the white perfection of your prayer
Is there, enveloping all things, until
The oneness of the One is everywhere.
Nothing remains the same—only the still,
Only the peace of being, not so much
Filling space as obliterating space,
An emptiness and allness, like the touch
Of snowfall in the night upon your face.
But when your prayer ends and you rise and go,
Your world shines new around you, like new
    snow.

Dear God,

This is a new beginning for me—not because something is happening to me, but because something miraculous is happening *within* me. Now I know that the yearning I have felt through-out life—a yearning that could not be fulfilled by anyone or anything—is satisfied only by being fully in Your presence through prayer.

You are the spirit of life that has been within me from the beginning. You encouraged me to take my first breath, and you were there saturating the very air that I took into my body. Every breath I have taken since then is both my celebration of Your presence and Your assurance that You are always with me, renewing me with the breath of life.

God, You have given me life, and every day can be a new beginning for me. Every day will be an adventure in living because I am ready to live life fully—in the awareness of You.

In this quiet time of prayer,
I celebrate the breath of life.

Some Journaling Ideas

—— ◆ ——

1. What can I do today to remind myself that even the simple act of breathing is a celebration of God's presence within me?
2. How can I be alert to new opportunities and new beginnings in my life?

"The big question is whether you are going to be able to say a hearty yes to your adventure."

—JOSEPH CAMPBELL

Immersed

By John D. Engle Jr.

Immersed in infinite energy and love,
I'm part of the eternal flow of things.
No matter when or where or how I move,
whether on earth with wheels or in air with
     wings,
I am a part of everything that is,
all that has been, or will ever be.
Designed by the dreams of all divinities,
all beauty and all truth are mixed in me.
Knowing this, I shed my shell of doubt,
until free in the freedom of the one Mind
and linked to laws of love, I go about
fulfilling that for which I was designed,
which is to sing myself and try to share
the loveliness of which I am aware.

Dear God,

I know that I don't have to wait for a formal time of prayer to reflect on Your blessings in my life. Every moment of my day is a spiritual experience when I understand that You are with me—and that Your love for me is boundless!

Thinking about You and my relationship with You—as a creation to the Creator—fills me with unquenchable joy! I am so glad to be alive, so glad to be a part of Your universe! Whether I am working or playing or simply resting in the awareness of Your presence within me, I feel connected with You, the source of life that gives me the energy I need to keep going.

You are with me now and every moment of my life. I am Your beloved creation, so if I should begin to feel overwhelmed with doubt, I know that I need only change my focus from whatever is troubling me to what is always the absolute truth about me: You, dear God, will see me through.

In this quiet time of prayer,
I give thanks for my blessings.

Some Journaling Ideas

— ◆ —

1. When do I feel most like a beloved creation of God?
2. How can I stay open today to seeing God in the little things in life?

Day 3
Discovery

"The only real voyage of discovery consists not in seeking new landscapes but in having new eyes."

—MARCEL PROUST

The Search

By Donna Miesbach

Here, within the quiet zone of inner space,
I find myself exploring, like those in days of old,
The potential of this vast uncharted sea
That harbors the meaning of existence.

Like all who've sought before me,
I can only grope within the confines of my soul,
And yet there seems to be a pull,
A gravitation toward some unseen inner light
    that says,
"Here! This is the way!"

And so I follow, fully aware
That no matter where it leads—
This is only the beginning.
I can never exhaust my potential;
Growth is forever.

And even when I've changed
To a state light-years away,
I will become yet more,
For it is in the search itself
That truth is revealed
As I encounter
The essence of my identity.

Dear God,

You have led me to this time and this place of discovery. And as I consider all that has happened to bring me to this sacred awakening, I understand that each time I pray I have opened the door to new opportunities—opportunities to discover more of my own spirituality. As I continue to explore these new paths, I realize my potential for being more and doing more.

Being totally in Your presence has revived the memory of a sacred bond that has always existed between us. As I pray, my spirit is rekindled, and I am so infused with faith that I welcome the chance to learn more of You and of what I am capable of achieving.

No longer do I need to know the "why" of things, for You are the answer to every question, the resolution to every dilemma, the source of all that matters.

As I explore new horizons, O God, I am simply rediscovering more of You.

In this quiet time of prayer, I open the door to new discoveries and new possibilities.

Some Journaling Ideas

———— ◆ ————

1. How can I explore new paths to spiritual awakening today?
2. In what ways has God already answered my call?

Day 4
—◆—
Acceptance

"God enters by a private door
into every individual."

—RALPH WALDO EMERSON

To Find the God We Seek

By Richard Rainbolt

And on his last day
The student said to the Master:
"You have shown me the wonders of life
And made me hear the winds of love
Rushing through the universe,
And helped me to understand
That God lives in all things;
Yet there is again something higher.
How do we find the God we seek?"

And the Master said,
"When all among the human kind
Focus their thoughts on God
At the same time,
They will create a universal oneness
That is the God they seek."

Dear God,

In my commitment to know more about You, I am also learning more about myself. Believing that Your unlimited power and wisdom can work through me, I am uncovering amazing insights at the very soul-level of my being. I realize that I have the ability to achieve my desires and goals. I simply must be willing to try.

And, God, with my acceptance of You as the source of understanding and life, I am aware of the divine ideas that are filtering through my thoughts and dreams. I understand that by never limiting myself, I will never limit what You can do through me.

Because I accept the honor of being a channel of Your spirit, a new *me* is constantly emerging—an unfolding creation of Your life and love. When I hold myself to this high standard, I realize that nothing is too good to be true. I accept You as the source of every blessing and invite blessing after blessing into my life.

In this quiet time of prayer, I recognize God as the source of all blessings.

Some Journaling Ideas

———◆———

1. What can I do today to recognize God's abundance in my life?
2. In what ways do I see a new *me* emerging?

Day 5
—◆—
Surrender

"*Do not let your hearts be troubled,
and do not let them be afraid.*"

—JESUS

The Answer

By Lowell Fillmore

When for a purpose
I had prayed and prayed and prayed
Until my words seemed worn and bare
    With arduous use.
And I had knocked and asked and knocked
    and asked again,
And all my fervor and persistence brought
    no hope,
I paused to give my weary brain a rest
And ceased my anxious human cry.
    In that still moment,
After self had tried and failed,
There came a glorious vision of God's power,
And, lo, my prayer was answered in that hour.

Dear God,

Sometimes it seems that the hardest thing I can do is to let go—even of the thoughts and circumstances that trouble me. Yet I know that letting go is what I must do for my own health and peace of mind.

So in this moment, I surrender all to Your healing love. In my heart and soul, I let go of what is worrying me and let Your sweet, divine will be my only desire.

I let go of worry, I let go of doubt, I let go of any situation that is causing me to feel concern or pain. I surrender these things to You, God, and know that I receive the soothing touch of Your loving presence in return.

As I surrender myself to You, I am filled with such a sense of peace—a peace that passes all human understanding. I know in my heart that as long as I surrender to Your will, all is well, all is working out according to Your divine plan.

In this quiet time of prayer, I surrender to the healing love of God.

Some Journaling Ideas

———◆———

1. What can I release to God for a divine outcome today?
2. How and where might I experience more of God's peace?

Day 6
—◆—
Reverence

"In the faces of men and women
I see God."

—WALT WHITMAN

This Quiet Place

By Dorothy Pierson

I came to this quiet place
And found You waiting for me, God.
I hadn't heard You call,
I had no seeming need at all,
But I just felt guided to be still . . .
And here You are!

My heart is open to Your will.
Speak to me, God,
For I am listening within myself.
I hear You in my mind,
A kind of moving
As in the quiet of a forest,
Pleasant sounds, soft and whispering
To my heart.
In this place apart, O God,
Thank You for the peace I feel,
The sure knowing that You are here,
And real,
And that we are one
In this quiet place.

Dear God,

   With a new awareness of both You and of myself, I am able to recognize the sacredness that I hold within me. I have tasted the sweetness of Your spirit and felt the joy of Your unqualified acceptance and love. I have breathed deeply of Your presence and I am refreshed in spirit.

   I am one with You and one with all creation. In mind and heart, I recognize You as the one universal spirit that unites all humankind and nature. Together, we are all woven into a beautiful tapestry of love, harmony, and understanding.

   Your love for all life resonates within me as a divine connection that can never be broken. I honor that sacred bond with the sanctity it is worthy of.

   O dear God, You are all that I could ever want and all that I will ever need.

In this quiet time of prayer, I connect with my own sacredness.

Some Journaling Ideas

—— ◆ ——

1. What is one way I may become more aware of my oneness with God today?
2. What is one thing I can do today to honor my sacred bond with others?

Day 7
◆
Renewal

"Dreams are renewable. No
matter what our age or condition,
there are still untapped possibilities
within us and new beauty
waiting to be born."

—DR. DALE TURNER

Renewal

By J. Sig Paulson

O Lord of renewal,
refresh me,
restore me,
renew me again.
Make me
newer than new
and brighter than bright,
and then
respond once more
to my joyous shout:
"Renew me forever from the inside out!"

Dear God,

I feel Your presence as renewing life within me—an energizing flow that surges throughout my body, healing me and making me aware that I am alive with divine life!

Knowing I am part of Your sacred presence, I feel renewed and vibrantly alive. The troubles of the day slip effortlessly from my mind when I am thinking only of You.

I bask in Your healing glow; Your love fills me with strength; Your presence renews me spiritually, emotionally, and physically.

God, Your spirit is within me—and I know this into the deepest recesses of my soul. So I am filled with the assurance that no matter where I may go, no matter what I may undertake, You are always with me.

You are the life that energizes me now!

In this quiet time of prayer, I feel renewed!

Some Journaling Ideas

——— ◆ ———

1. When do I feel most renewed and refreshed?
2. How do I feel when I focus on the energy of God moving through me?

"Faith is love taking the form of aspiration."

—WILLIAM ELLERY CHANNING

A Parable

By Mildred N. Hoyer

Observe
The faith of a caterpillar
That never questions "why."
Behold
What was a homely worm
Becomes a butterfly.

Dear God,

I have a great desire to live my life as You created me to live it—as a spiritual being. Although I am going through the human experience, I know I am always part of You. In the past, I may have limited myself by what I thought I lacked as a person, but now I know the great possibility I have inherited as Your creation.

And this is such an important understanding, because now I won't let my humanness get in the way of my spirituality. I am freeing myself to be who I truly am and to do what I can truly do. It's as if the positive thought "With God, I can," were whispering quietly, gently to me throughout the day—every day.

The language of Your spirit speaks as the voice I recognize and follow, no matter what is happening around me. Even if my day seems out of order, I know there is a divine order at work in me and through me. As I listen for Your blessed encouragement, I hear You whisper, "With Me, you can."

In this quiet time of prayer, I affirm the truth: I am a spiritual being!

Some Journaling Ideas

——— ◆ ———

1. How can I more fully know that I am a spiritual being living a human experience?
2. What assurance do I receive that God is always with me?

"Look at everything as though you were seeing it either for the first or last time. Then your time on Earth will be filled with glory."

—BETTY SMITH

Ripples

By Verle Bell

Scholars tell us
　　that a stone,
　　　　dropped into still water,
　　　　　　causes ripples whose effect
　　　　　　　　goes on eternally . . .
　　Their vibration never ceases.

Sages have said
　　that one loving thought,
　　　　cast into the sea of life,
　　　　　　has infinite value . . .
　　Its vital waves go on
　　　　and on and on, blending
　　　　　　with other loving thoughts,
　　　　　　　　strengthening, intensifying,
　　multiplying their immortal good.

Dear God,

As I watch the dawn slowly breaking across the morning sky, bathing Earth with warming rays of light, I feel an awareness of Your spirit rising within me. Filled with an unmistakable sense of You, I cannot nor will not turn away from the beauty of Your light—the light within me and the world.

I see people and situations through spiritual vision. I see all people as You intended them to be—there is no race, no age, no gender. There is only love, for we are all Your love in expression.

I do more than simply desire to be one with Your light; I express it as understanding and love so that I can hold on to the reality of my oneness with You in every moment. I have seen Your glory, and now I live it and express it in my life.

Dear God, I am Your glory in action. I magnify Your presence by sharing with others—through my words and actions—the message of Your love.

In this quiet time of prayer, I immerse myself in the light and love of God.

Some Journaling Ideas

———◆———

1. How do I express more love and understanding toward myself and others?
2. What can I do today to infuse my oneness with God into all my activities?

Day 10
—◆—
Transformation

*"Don't go through life;
GROW through life."*

—ERIC BUTTERWORTH

Transformation

By R. H. Grenville

In winter these hills were deep
in silence; noon, a hazy glow
beyond bare trees that rose above
the beauty of unblemished snow.

In summer we can scarce believe
the transformation! Everywhere,
flowers and leaves, a laughing brook
we never could have dreamed was there;
the song of birds, the scent of pine
the new-mown hay, and something more:
a gentle, lovely parable
of life's great power to restore,
renew, transform, create, repair
what, for a while, seemed bleak and bare.

Dear God,

You show me such wonders all along this journey called life! As I look within the mirror of my soul, I see my true reflection: a spiritual being. With a vision for the divine, I see beyond the physical to the core of my being—the creation that I am.

God, there is so much more wonder awaiting me than what I have experienced so far on this journey. Your promise of eternal love, joy, and peace assures me of that. During my times of prayer and meditation, I have learned to move far beyond what may appear to be and on to the un-limited possibilities that lie before me. With You, all things are possible.

I am continually being transformed into a clearer image of Your greatness, and my heart leaps with joy. I, too, am a wonder of Your creativity!

In this quiet time of prayer,
I experience the wonder of God.

Some Journaling Ideas

——◆——

1. What are some of the wonders I have seen or may see today?
2. How do I show appreciation for the beauty in my life?

EXPRESSING
SPIRITUAL
QUALITIES

HONORING OUR
SPIRITUALITY IN PRAYER

BY JACKIE NINK PFLUG, AUTHOR AND MOTIVATOR

I had been returning to my teaching job in Cairo, Egypt, from a trip to Greece when the EgyptAir plane on which I was a passenger was hijacked. The plane was now parked on the runway of an airport in Malta. Several passengers had been shot and killed by the terrorists because their demand for fuel to reach their destination was not being met.

I was next, but I felt no fear—only overwhelming love as I began to picture in my mind the sweet, familiar faces of family and friends. One by one, I told them good-bye.

As I was led up the aisle of the plane, I silently prayed the Lord's Prayer. When I reached the door of the plane, an explosion went off in my head and then a heaviness spread throughout my body. I felt as if I were floating in air, but I was actually tumbling down the metal staircase onto the tarmac. I stayed conscious only long enough to realize something incredible: I was still alive!

In fact, I was one of the few passengers to live, for a few hours later, a rescue attempt was made and many of the passengers were killed. When the medics picked me up off the tarmac, they thought I was dead. But in the ambulance, one of them turned me over, and I gasped for air. Immediately, they changed our destination—from the morgue to the hospital.

Yes, I was alive, but I was also left with hearing, sight,

46

and memory impairments. In the next few years, I needed prayer and faith, friends, doctors, and therapists to help me through to a healing. A friend who had discovered her own spirituality encouraged me to listen to my own inner voice for guidance. As I spent more and more time in prayer, in silence with God, I noticed a calming, comforting feeling growing within me.

As I gradually improved, I began to think about what I had learned from my experience: I had faced death without fear, and I found a strength and a faith I never dreamed I had. I also discovered that God's spirit is within me, that I can never be separated from the loving presence and power of God.

In my new role as a motivational speaker, I tell people what they already intuitively know is true: Blessings really do come from what appear to be challenges. I encourage them to pray, to talk to God as a friend. I encourage them to embrace the truth that is true for us all: When we honor our own spirituality, we discover the answers to our prayers and have the courage to claim them.

*"All, everything that I understand,
I understand only because I love."*

—LEO TOLSTOY

Love

By James Dillet Freeman

Love may sometimes be a light thing—
    You may wear it like a flower
Or a ring upon your finger—
    Yet love has lasting power.
But whether love lights lightly
    Or for eternity,
You find the more it binds you,
    The more it sets you free.
Love may sometimes lay a heavy load
    You think you cannot bear,
But love and you together
    Have strength enough to spare.
Love lifts you on invisible
    But ah, what mighty wings!
When life is dearest and most blest,
    Love is the song it sings.

Dear God,

Your love is unlike any other love I have ever known. My parents, friends, and others are all influenced by human emotions, and they may have given or withheld love at will. But Your love for me is unconditional, without judgment, without limitation.

There are no conditions I must meet or exceed to earn Your love. I express my faith in You by returning love in the form of thanksgiving and appreciation and by respecting and showing my love for all You have created.

I know that I may come to a crossroads as I walk my path in life. Because You love me, You have given me the freedom to make choices and to express my faith. My Creator, I turn to You for guidance and support and receive love and encouragement.

O God, You are my God, and I love You.

In this quiet time of prayer, I feel God's loving presence and let God love through me!

Some Journaling Ideas

—◆—

1. What is one way I can express God's love in my life today?
2. How do I feel when I remember all that God has so lovingly created in my life?

Day 12
—◆—
Inner Peace

*"Do you want an impenetrable
sense of inner peace? Take a deep
breath . . . let go of anxiety . . .
ask God to lift the clouds of doubt
and fear from your vision. Believe
that peace is your natural state."*

—CHRISTOPHER H. JACKSON

I Am There

By James Dillet Freeman

Do you need Me?
I am there.
You cannot see Me, yet I am the light
    you see by.
You cannot hear Me, yet I speak through
    your voice.
You cannot feel Me, yet I am the power at
    work in your hands.
I am at work, though you do not understand
    My ways.
I am at work, though you do not recognize
    My works.
I am not strange visions. I am not mysteries.
Only in absolute stillness, beyond self, can
    you know Me as I am, and then but as a
    feeling and a faith.
Yet I am there. Yet I hear. Yet I answer.
When you need Me, I am there.

Dear God,

As I allow myself to feel the inner peace that is always within me, I know how it feels to be peace-filled. As gently as a summer breeze, Your peace soothes my hurts and eases my fears.

I relax completely into Your peace. My awareness of Your presence warms my heart and encourages me to leave all confusion behind as I linger here with You.

Calmly, quietly, peace settles over me, wrapping me in a cocoon that insulates me from stress. Enfolded in divine peace, I am safe and secure.

God, this peace is more than the absence of stress; it is absolute serenity. It is a peace that I share with others, a peace that invites me to seek You even more.

Knowing You are here with me, I am comforted, for with You, dear God, I *am* peace.

In this quiet time of prayer, I relax and let the peace of God wash over me.

Some Journaling Ideas

— ◆ —

1. When I am at peace, how do I feel?
2. How can I more fully live from a true sense of peace today?

Day 13
—◆—
Understanding

*"Nothing in life is to be feared.
It is only to be understood."*

—MARIE CURIE

Knowing

By Verle Bell

It is a point just beyond
  wondering, doubting, waiting;
 A certainty that *now* is the time for
  a bud to uncurl;
 An undeniable urge in the swallow
  that this is the instant to rise
   in flight toward the south;
 A realization in the cells
  that *now* is the moment for
   a wound to begin to heal;
 The moment when a soul decides it is time
  to move on to a new realm.
Knowing comes from within
  and cannot be denied.
Thank You, God, that I know You are,
   That I know You are love,
  And that I know I am Yours.

Dear God,

You have spoken and I have listened. Because You have taught me the beauty of unconditional love, I recognize Your essence in *all* people—not just my family and friends. Your spirit is within all!

And God, I know I cannot hold on to that feeling of pure love without first making compassion and understanding a daily practice. Then I go beyond *saying* that I am understanding of others—I *live* my life so that understanding is an everyday part of my life.

I do not condemn others for their words or actions. Rather, I let my interactions with them be an opportunity to be completely nonjudgmental. Each time I am understanding of others, *I* understand how it feels to be an expression of Your compassion.

I thank You for the opportunity, God.

In this quiet time of prayer, I build understanding and compassion that are divine in nature.

Some Journaling Ideas

——— ◆ ———

1. How can I be more understanding and show more compassion to others today?
2. How will I encourage myself to see God in all people?

Day 14
◆
Life

*"Don't do things to not die,
do things to enjoy living.
The by-product may be not dying."*

—Bernie S. Siegel, M.D.

Portrait of a Life

By Elaine Meyer

A portrait of my life
Hangs before me now.
It was painted by the Master—
Each stroke made with love.
To date it remains unfinished,
Yet worked on day by day,
Continually unfolding,
Revealing my divine destiny.
Only the Master will complete
The portrait of my life,
For only the Master knows
The strokes yet to be made.

Dear God,

It's true: I have never felt more alive than I do now. And this is because I know that I am more than physically alive. I am also spiritually alive! I am alive with the flame of Your spirit, which is an inner beacon that draws me home to my reality—my spirituality. You are the source of life—life that is everlasting and fulfilling.

Yes, God, I am alive with the same energy that powers the universe! Sunshine warming my face is a silent reminder that You move as invisible but all-powerful energy in all and through all. And the miracle of it is that You have given me life and You are also constantly renewing me.

With my whole self—spirit, mind, and body—I give expression to life and healing. And I do this according to Your divine plan, which you have so lovingly written on my heart.

Oh, how alive I am with Your life, God!

In this quiet time of prayer, I am renewed and revitalized. I am spiritually alive!

Some Journaling Ideas

—— ◆ ——

1. How do I feel knowing that the spark of divine life is within me?
2. What can I do today to be aware that I am not only physically but also spiritually alive?

Day 15
—◆—
Joy

*"We can't become what we need
to be by remaining what we are."*

—OPRAH WINFREY

The Music of Prayer

By Florence A. Hawn

On a leaf-strewn path one day
There, in the woods, I paused to pray.
Through the silence could be heard
The rustle of leaves and chirping birds.
It was like a minisymphony,
A prayer time filled with harmony.
No words outspoken could express
My inner joy and thankfulness
For music that was so divine
And told me answered prayer was mine.

Dear God,

Every day—no matter how unusual or routine, no matter how much I have learned or unlearned—is a new time of growth and understanding for me. Then, so quickly, today turns into yesterday and a new day gently nudges me forward.

What is becoming so clear, God, is that *I* can choose what to bring with me to each new day. *I* can decide what I give to each fresh, new experience. *I choose joy.* I can always give from the joy that You are within me, because You are the *one* constant in my life. I cannot help but feel joy in sensing Your presence.

I feel the joy of Your spirit within as it lives out through me. This kind of joy is more than an emotion of happiness; it is a feeling of wholeness that cannot be contained. It is a joy that builds on itself. As if in a great rush, I learned how to walk, then to run—and now I have discovered that I can soar!

My heart soars with the joy of spirit!

In this quiet time of prayer, I choose to experience pure joy.

Some Journaling Ideas

———◆———

1. What can I do today to express more of the joy that is within me?
2. When I choose to bring joy to this day, how might that affect my relationships with others?

Day 16
—◆—
Harmony

"Be the living expression of God's kindness; kindness in your face, kindness in your eyes, kindness in your warm greeting."

—MOTHER TERESA

Reaching Out

By Winifred Brand

My spirit wants to reach
and stretch and grow,
to go beyond the fears and hunger
and the disillusions
of the world we know.
And yet I know
it cannot reach
and stretch
and grow
beyond the aching of the soul,
until it takes
the fears
the hopes
the tears
the doubts and shattered dreams
unto itself,
resolving every one
in its own way
and reaching first
the Spirit within.

Dear God,

Your spirit within me sounds a note of accord. Your presence within creates a reservoir of harmony that unites me with others in love.

My heart beats in time with the harmony of the universe, and I am filled with a sense of being an important part of the whole. I am in tune with Your loving spirit, and I am vitally alive!

I am alive and in tune with the harmony of all life! And I create more harmony by staying focused on You, for You are the unconditional love that unites me with others.

God, You are the inspiration behind every loving word I speak. You are the source of joy I feel as I live my life in harmony and love. I can be an instrument of divine harmony each time I trust You to show me how.

My faith is in You.

In this quiet time of prayer, I tune in to the harmony of the universe and find my inspiration.

Some Journaling Ideas

—— ◆ ——

1. What important contribution can I make toward harmonizing my world?
2. How can I become more in tune with God's loving spirit today?

_____

_____

_____

_____

_____

_____

_____

_____

_____

_____

_____

_____

_____

_____

"Humanity is never so beautiful as when . . . forgiving another."

—JEAN PAUL RICHTER

Bridges

By James Dillet Freeman

When we come to rivers,
We look for bridges—
Most of us come to rivers
That we have to cross.

A bridge may be a person,
Someone dear, or sometimes a stranger;
A bridge may be an incident,
Planned, or sometimes happenstance;
A bridge may be a prayer.

Dear God, I do not pray
That there may be no rivers,
But please, God, I would like
for there to be a bridge or two.

Dear God,

I may have been reminded by my parents, teachers, and peers to forgive and forget. But You have guided me beyond that and reminded me that, in any situation, You are with me to heal and support me.

I no longer look to the past with a sense of regret. The truth is that my happiness lies in the present with You, sweet Spirit, and I no longer have to hide from past hurts. I can face them and accept them as lessons I have learned, and then move on.

I look at the world and all that happens in it through eyes of forgiveness, not fear or judgment. And when I do this, I do not judge others harshly or allow their words or actions to hurt me.

I also forgive myself for what I have done or left undone. The truth of my existence is in You, dear God.

In this quiet time of prayer, I let go of the past and forgive.

Some Journaling Ideas

———◆———

1. Do I have any past regret that I need to let go of today?
2. What benefits will I reap from the act of forgiveness?

"I thank God for my handicaps, for through them I have found myself, my work, and my God."

—HELEN KELLER

Arise and Shine!

By R. H. Grenville

Arise and shine, like the sun.
You and the Light of Life are one!
As light adds sparkle to the dew,
Love's holy fire enlivens you
with power to know, and do, and be.
Not separate and falling free
through cloudy chance, but born of Light,
a human star in your own right,
forever one with the Divine,
God's precious child!
So rise and shine!

Dear God,

I know that You are always with me, yet there may be times when I feel as if *I* do not have what it takes to go on, that *I* just do not have the strength or courage to do what I must do. So today, I am making it my resolve to trust *You*, to lean on *You*, to have faith in *You*.

Your spirit is within me, God, a nourishing life-force that flows throughout my body. As I give You my complete trust, I begin to feel *Your* mighty strength. This gives me the power to be who I am meant to be—who You created me to be.

You give me the courage to be true to myself, true to my divine heritage. I realize that no person or circumstance can take away what You have given me, for You are the source of all there is.

Dear God, I welcome each new opportunity to express the life and power that You are within me. I actually feel Your strength rising within me now.

In this quiet time of prayer, I am filled
with power!

Some Journaling Ideas

—— ◆ ——

1. How can I use spiritual power wisely today?
2. In what ways do I express my divine heritage of strength?

"Things are beautiful if you love them."

—JEAN ANOUILH

Through the Eyes of Love

By James Dillet Freeman

Can you see the flowers when no flowers are
    there?
When the sky is empty and the fields are bare,
Can you see the beauty? Try, and you may feel
Through mind's thin curtain to the eternal real
And shining glory, see the way things look
As they are painted in God's picture book,
See that the stuff things have been fashioned of
Is not dull clay, but luminous with the love
Of God, and everywhere around you lies
Heaven, when you look at it with love's eyes.
Not even all the flowers of May can match
This wonderment. Look, look, and you may
    catch
Glimpses of what was in God's heart and mind
When first He made the world—oh, beautiful
    and kind!

Dear God,

Everywhere I look I see the beauty of Your creation, and I am filled with awe as I behold the wonder of all that You are. Your creativity is evident in everything—from the smallest to the most magnificent of organisms—and that includes me as well.

Your spirit fills me, dear God, and is the beauty of my soul. I *am* beautiful because I am Your creation. And it is the spark of Your divinity within me that makes me worthy of the best, worthy of the greatest care and consideration.

I never want to be less than who You inspire me to be, so I let Your beauty shine forth in everything I do. I am loving, I am kind, and I treat everyone else with the respect they deserve as Your beloved creations.

Your divine spirit is shining brightly from me, and I am warmed by the glow of its beauty.

In this quiet time of prayer, I thank God for the beauty of the universe.

Some Journaling Ideas

———◆———

1. How can I more fully appreciate the beauty of the world around me?
2. How can I more fully understand my true beauty of spirit?

Day 20
—◆—
Freedom

"Freedom is nothing else but a chance to be better."

—ALBERT CAMUS

No Other Way

By Martha Smock

Could we but see the pattern of our days,
We should discern how devious were the ways
By which we came to this, the present time,
This place in life; and we should see the climb
Our soul has made up through the years.
We should forget the hurts, the wanderings,
     the fears,
The wastelands of our life, and know
That we could come no other way or grow
Into our good without these steps our feet
Found hard to take, our faith found hard to
     meet.
The road of life winds on, and we like
     travelers go
From turn to turn until we come to know
The truth that life is endless and that we
Forever are inhabitants of all eternity.

Dear God,

What freedom I know when I let Your power live out through me to break any habit or tendency that has limited me! It's amazing, but when I give up the struggle between "I can" and "I can't" and trust in Your power, I am filled with new strength and conviction.

My faith in You starts a new conversation that goes something like this: "With You, God, I can!" I don't hit the panic button if a nagging doubt tries to make a comeback. I simply speak Your name silently or quietly and I feel more confident.

So, God, thank You for always being here for me, for listening to every prayer, for giving me assurance through the stirring within my soul. I have the freedom to be the strong, confident, com-passionate person I am capable of being.

I am free!

In this quiet time of prayer, a whole new world of possibilities opens up to me.

Some Journaling Ideas

———— ◆ ————

1. What are the ways in which I feel free? What can I do to enhance this feeling?
2. How might I express my newfound freedom of spirit?

_____

_____

_____

_____

_____

_____

_____

_____

_____

_____

_____

_____

_____

HEALING THE WHOLE PERSON

SURRENDERING
TO LOVE
BY GERALD G. JAMPOLSKY, M.D.

I was an atheist for most of my life. But in 1975, I underwent a spiritual transformation. I was feeling the pressure of being a doctor, and at the same time, I was going through a painful divorce. I was killing myself with alcohol, yet I was also afraid to die.

One day, while making rounds at the hospital, I overheard a child—a cancer patient—ask his doctor a question that had been on my mind, too: "What is it like to die?" Not honoring the trust this child placed in him, the doctor ignored the question and changed the subject.

At that moment, I began my search to find out what happens to children in the hospital when they ask such a question. Whom could they trust? I found that many times the only person they could turn to for love and support was the cleaning lady who came into their rooms every morning.

I began to pray and received the guidance to start a center to help children deal with their questions. It is a free center for attitudinal healing for children who are suffering from catastrophic illnesses such as cancer, leukemia, and AIDS. What I soon discovered, though, was that these children were wise spirits in young bodies. They taught me not to be afraid of death and that our purpose here on Earth is to love and forgive.

At the center, we define *health* as inner peace and *healing* as letting go of fear. We have a number of principles we teach, and the first one is that the very essence of our beings is love.

And we can all have hope because God is always with us, because we are one in spirit, because life is eternal, and because there is love.

Love is an experience beyond definition—as difficult to define as God is. Love is unconditional and never ceases. It never judges, and it is the timeless answer to every problem, every sickness, every pain. Love is the answer.

Surrendering to love, surrendering to God, is what life is all about, and this is what I am here to learn and hopefully to demonstrate. So I do my best to make each moment a prayer on my pathway home to God.

"One's own thought is one's world. What a person thinks is what he becomes."

—MAITRI UPANISHAD

For Healing

By R. H. Grenville

Come, step into the pool
of quietness.
Relax your tired heart.
Let silence bless
and ease your every part
to tranquil trust,
washing away all trace
of weary dust.
This quiet holds the calm
of silken seas.
Enter it gratefully
and take your ease.
An angel Presence
ministers to all
who seek
this timeless place.
Her name is Peace.

Dear God,

For the most part, I think about healing when I have some condition that I think needs to be healed. Yet I know that healing of my body is a natural, everyday occurrence that quietly goes about following Your blueprint of health for me. You, Master Creator, are the one source of all life and healing.

I am a whole being with an immune system that not only knows what is pure and authentic to me but also neutralizes all that is impure within me. As I give thanks for my immune system, I am saying *yes* to its continued good work.

No matter who or what seems to aid in my healing or the healing of others, You are the source of it all. You are the creator of all life and the renewal within all life. You are the divine ideal behind every new treatment that soothes and heals the human condition. Oh, *yes*, God of creation, You are the source of all life and healing.

I say *yes* to Your healing life!

In this quiet time of prayer, I commune with God, the source of all life.

Some Journaling Ideas

——— ◆ ———

1. How is divine life expressing through me now?
2. What can I do to feel refreshed and renewed at any time of the day?

Day 22
◆
Changing Thoughts

"When you set out on a journey
and night covers the road, you
don't conclude that the road has
vanished. . . . How else could we
discover the stars?"

—UNKNOWN

Guidance

By R. H. Grenville

Behold the spinner of the dawn:
how fine her fragile threads are drawn,
without a pattern or a plan
apparent to the eyes of man.

Shall wisdom, that could so impart
tuition to a spider's heart
to form this lacy filigree,
in time of need, not tutor me?

Shall this, the pattern of my days,
not yet evolve in lovely ways,
revealing, when the whole is shown,
a purpose greater than my own?

Dear God,

In my prayers and times of silence, You have shown me the blessings that I already have and the promise of a whole lifetime of blessings. You have also shown me that, although I am always in Your care and keeping, You give me the opportunity to work with You in shaping my own life. You have blessed me with the responsibility of making my own choices.

God, with Your support and encouragement, I make one of those choices today. I choose not to become so caught up in healing my physical body that I forget my spiritual well-being.

A positive, healthy spirit is vital to enjoying a truly healthy body. By thinking positive thoughts and keeping focused on my oneness with You, I create a healthy environment in which both spiritual and physical healing take place.

In this quiet time of prayer, I create the perfect environment for spiritual and physical healing.

Some Journaling Ideas

—— ◆ ——

1. What is spiritual health? What is physical health?
2. What positive actions can I take today that will promote spiritual healing?

*"In the middle of every difficulty
lies opportunity."*

—ALBERT EINSTEIN

Expectation

By Dorothy Pierson

O God,
I will enjoy this day!
My expectation is of good.
I am open to the new
Though it may not yet be
Understood.

If I find myself in a place
I have not been before,
Though I cannot see the outcome,
I will trust You even more.

Today I set my mind
In tune with Your loving care.
I will enjoy this day
And look for You
Everywhere!

Dear God,

You are the joy that refreshes me when I become tired. You are the peace that soothes me when I am feeling stressed. You are the hope that lifts me up when I feel discouraged. God, knowing that You are always with me assures me that there is a way.

So I let go of hurts and fears and let Your spirit within me clear away any thought that does not contribute to a feeling of contentment or well-being. You accept me as I am, God, so I need never fear that You will withhold any blessing.

I am filled with Your presence. So I can let go of any worry or doubt and know that with You, God, nothing is impossible. I have nothing to fear, for nothing can take away the happiness I derive from being aware of You.

In mind, body, and spirit, I am truly a whole and healthy being.

In this quiet time of prayer, I am healed in mind, body, and spirit.

Some Journaling Ideas

— ◆ —

1. What can I do today to make it easier for me to let go of emotional pain?
2. In what ways do I recognize that God is always with me?

Day 24
◆
Physical Healing

"I have learned never to underestimate the healing power we all have. It is always there to be used for the highest good. We just have to remember to use it."

—MARK VICTOR HANSEN

Healing

By Serene S. West

Does a healing come in a twinkling light?
Or could it begin with a smile?
Does a healing come with a thunderous roar?
Or does it sometimes take awhile?

I've seen healings birth under doctor's care,
Yet I've seen them come in a flash!
But I know that all healings come from pure
    love—
In abundance—for all who would ask!

Dear God,

I may not have always appreciated the master-piece that my body is, but my appreciation is growing. I realize that what I may have thought of as imperfections are the features that make me unique.

I sense an inaudible message being repeated to me: "You, my beloved, were not cast from a mold. You are like no other person who ever was or ever will be. Know this truth for yourself and for all others. Everyone in existence was formed from my love. So live your uniqueness now."

And, God, I feel I am not mistaken in believing that this is Your message about me and to me—about all others and to them also. I appreciate my own sacredness and the sacredness of each person. I shall never again look upon one of Your creations without beholding the beauty and wonder of Your love.

In this quiet time of prayer, I am aware that I am a unique creation of God's sacred design.

Some Journaling Ideas

———◆———

1. What will I do today to celebrate my own unique qualities?
2. How do I look at others in order to appreciate their unique spiritual nature?

*"Where there is great love,
there are always miracles."*

—WILLA CATHER

Together

By Dorothy Pierson

Together we grow,
Not separate, divided,
Alone, or in isolation.
We grow best
When we come to know
That at the core of being,
We are so much more!
We are one with every living soul,
Every atom, every cell,
Every living, moving thing,
As well as so-called static form . . .
All a part of us and we of them!
For we are born and grow
In a wholeness we come to know
As love.
And in that love
God holds us all,
Together.

Dear God,

I am discovering more and more that each day is a process of continual healing. Although my mind is positive and my body is physically healthy, it is essential that I keep my energies focused on You and Your healing love as I interact with others.

Sweet Spirit, my hope and prayer is that I know Your presence at all times as intimately as I do in this moment. This is my prayer for loved ones, too. I pray that individually and collectively we feel a peace that words cannot describe, a love that knows no boundaries.

Thank You, God, for the blessing of these people, for they are beautiful expressions of You. Indeed, the greatest gift I have ever known is the capacity to love—to love You, to love myself, and to love others.

In this quiet time of prayer, I receive the gift of love.

Some Journaling Ideas

——◆——

1. What seems to enhance my relationships with all people?
2. How can I express more of God's love in my life?

Day 26
Goals

*"I like the dreams of the future
better than the history of the past."*

—Thomas Jefferson

The Journey of Today

By James Dillet Freeman

Dawn is the threshold of today.
Dawn is an open door
That sends you up a sunlit way
You have not climbed before.
But you know God does not give
You hills too hard to climb;
God's love ordains that you shall live
But one day at a time.
Let go dead yesterday's regret,
Tomorrow's phantom fear;
Live in the living now and let
The present good appear.
Even a stay-at-home must make
The journey of today;
Go with a willing heart and take
Love's lamp to light your way;
Prayer be the staff you lean upon;
With faith your feet be shod.
Today you do not walk alone—
Today you walk with God.

Dear God,

I turn to You in prayer, knowing that You guide me to right paths so that I can do what is mine to do. God, I know that wherever You lead me is the perfect place for me to learn and grow and achieve the fulfillment for which I long.

Whatever my goals may be, the most important thing I could ever desire is to know You—to feel Your loving presence all around me and to see a glimpse of You in every person who greets me.

I seek You, God, and You show me the way to completion. And as I actively participate in each of life's grand adventures, I am continuing on a journey that will take me to experiences of the mind and heart that will strengthen my faith and provide me with breakthroughs to new growth.

Wherever I am right now is where I need to be. I thank You, God, for directing me here and for being here with me.

In this quiet time of prayer, God reveals my way.

Some Journaling Ideas

—◆—

1. What are the goals that I have achieved, and what goals do I have for the future?
2. How do I go about seeking a greater awareness of God's presence in me and around me?

"Praying is a very simple activity and requires no special words— only the willingness, the hunger, to know God."

—MARY-ALICE AND RICHARD JAFOLLA

About Prayer

By Mildred N. Hoyer

When all has been done that can be done,
    Though this, to some, may seem very odd,
The paramount need appears to be
    Just letting go, and letting God.

It's like closing the door, wrapping oneself
    In a kind of solitary pod,
And there in faith-filled quietness
    Just letting go, and letting God.

No need to struggle or plead the prayer,
    For when mind and heart no longer plod,
Amazingly, the answer comes—
    Just letting go, and letting God.

Dear God,

I am so filled with life during my talks with You each day! Whether I actually speak words or commune with You in silence, I feel enlivened! It's as if I were being recharged with new energy when I think about You or talk to You. Drawing on Your invisible power, I experience tangible and visible results. I am strengthened physically, emotionally, and spiritually.

The more I pray, the more I am blessed, and I've noticed a difference in how I feel. It's a miracle! Under the same stressful conditions I have had in the past, I now feel at peace. I have more compassion for and understanding of the people with whom I live and work. And I can even see the humor in situations that once caused me only discomfort.

God, talking to You is the most important part of the day. And what a comfort I receive in knowing that You are always waiting and ready to listen to me. Even when I am not calling, You keep the line of communication open to me. Thank You, God.

In this quiet time of prayer, I am blessed by my daily talks with God.

Some Journaling Ideas

———◆———

1. What am I going to say to God in my prayers today?
2. When I listen to God, what do I hear?

"In every community, there is work to be done. In every nation, there are wounds to heal. In every heart, there is the power to do it."

—MARIANNE WILLIAMSON

Make Me a Blessing, Lord

By James Dillet Freeman

Make me a blessing, Lord! Help me
To help those needing help, to be
A blessing to my fellow men.
Instruct me when to speak and when
To hold my speech, when to be bold
In giving and when to withhold;
And if I have not strength enough,
Then give me strength. Lord, make me tough
With my own self but tender toward
All others. Let there be outpoured
On me the gentleness to bless
All who have need of gentleness.
Give me a word, a touch to fill
The lonely life, faith for the ill,
And courage to keep hearts up though
My own is feeling just as low.
When men have bitter things to meet
And quail and would accept defeat,
Then let me lift their eyes to see
The vision of Thy victory.
Help me to help; help me to give
The wisdom and the will to live!

Dear God,

As I pray for my community, I pray that You will use me as an instrument of Your harmony and goodwill. With every cell of my being, I wish to be a channel for Your love. I want to be able to express love to everyone.

I start with the people I know—family and friends and neighbors—and then expand my vision to include others.

As I open myself to You, I feel Your love in every particle of my being. And it is Your love that helps me reach out to others—in my family, in my circle of friends, in my own community.

With every loving thought or word of encouragement, I am helping my community—I am helping to create a community in which peace and hope and kindness prevail because Your love always prevails.

In this quiet time of prayer, I give thanks for my community of family, friends, and neighbors.

Some Journaling Ideas

—— ◆ ——

1. What can I do to make my community stronger and
   more supportive?
2. How might changing myself—my actions and
   attitudes—initiate changes in my community?

"The soil, in return for her service,
keeps the tree tied to her;
the sky asks nothing and
leaves it free."

—RABINDRANATH TAGORE

All in All

By R. H. Grenville

All the petals of all the flowers,
all the minutes of all the hours,
all the waves of all the seas,
all the leaves of all the trees,
all the stars and all the brooks
are but a fraction of a part
of what life's great and giving heart
pours forth for us at love's decree:
God's infinite prosperity.

Dear God,

I am on a course set for healing—healing for myself and the world around me. This journey has become my mission now—to help anyone I can to know the peace found through healing love. And my mission continues by including all creation in my prayers.

You have taught me the sacredness of all life. You have shown me the way to love and be loved, the way to teach and be taught, the way to live and act in harmony with all life.

Life is a continuing process of creation, and I have a responsibility to all life. Earth is teeming with life in all shapes and sizes, and as I interact with these natural wonders, I allow You, God, to work through me, to do what is best for all Earth's inhabitants.

In this quiet time of prayer, I dedicate myself to helping the environment.

Some Journaling Ideas

— ◆ —

1. What can I do to help the environment in which I live?
2. How am I blessed by being a blessing in the world?

"You must be the change you wish
to see in the world."

—MAHATMA GANDHI

The Healing Heart

By Elaine Meyer

"The healing heart begins at home,"
She whispered in the baby's ear,
"Within your soul there lies a key
To a world of love without the fear.

"My child, I know a time will come
When joy of heart will change all things:
People living in harmony
With peace that pure divine love brings.

"Peace begins with you, dear heart,
And one day we will see our world be healed;
For divine love is the secret
Through which new worlds are revealed."

Dear God,

The news I read, see, and hear—what is happening to humankind the world over—is often sad. I may feel confused about what I can do to help heal the world of anger, disease, and conflict. Should I turn away and ignore it all?

Then, even when I am not seeking You and a divine answer, You somehow get through to me. Suddenly, the answer comes: I can pray for the healing of the world! It doesn't matter that I have never met the person I am praying for or been in the country where people are challenged. Your spirit within each of us connects us in the most powerful way people can be connected.

I pray for the healing of a child or an adult, for whole masses of people in cities or regions, and know that I am doing something powerfully good. By talking and acting in ways that encourage the healing of the world—of each person in the world—I live the truth of my prayers each day.

In this quiet time of prayer, I bless people all over the world with healing prayers.

Some Journaling Ideas

—— ◆ ——

1. What can I do to encourage the healing of the world?
2. How can my life be a blessing to all the people of the world?

LIVING FROM THE SACRED SOUL

AWAKENING TO GOD

BY DUKE TUFTY, MINISTER

I lay there on the bathroom floor of a motel room in Florida and counted the tiles. I needed to concentrate on something—anything except the fact that my life was slipping away. I had overdosed on cocaine, and my heart was beating wildly. I felt a tremendous temptation to close my eyes and move into unconsciousness, but I knew that if I did, I would never wake up again.

As the firstborn son of an affluent businessman in Sioux Falls, South Dakota, I never lacked for any material thing. And I was groomed from an early age to take over my father's successful car dealership when he retired.

My true nature—the life that *I* wanted to live—was bypassed. I was taught to ignore my inner desires and follow the outer desires of other people in order to fill my position in the family and in the family business. And in doing so, I felt no sense of being alive, no passion or joy.

I had no religion, no God. Life became very painful for me, and I wanted something that would numb the pain. I found it in alcohol and started to drink on a daily basis when I was seventeen. Eventually, I began to experiment with drugs and soon became addicted to cocaine. I fell into the pits of despair. . . .

As I lay on the cold tile floor that evening, I prayed: "God, just let me live. I will do anything. I don't want to die." All of a sudden, I recognized that my whole life had been a false, pretentious story. I had never been myself; I had always been some person I was trained to be. But even after I lost everything—the family business, my wife, and my children—I still was not myself. I was this drug-controlled person whom I did not want to be.

And yet, cocaine served as a bridge—from being the person who *had* existed to one who experienced a spiritual rebirth. The cocaine created the death, the final release of that old life, and surviving the overdose was a birth into a whole new existence. I made it through the night, and that was the last time I ever used cocaine.

I began a spiritual search, which eventually led to my becoming a Unity minister. And ministering to people who are in recovery is a big part of my ministry, but I know from my own personal experience that no one but the alcoholic or drug addict can make the decision to begin on the road to recovery.

The good news is that each of us has a spiritual nature. That nature needs to be expressed. When we get in touch with our spirituality—God's spirit within—we realize our true natures. And in that moment, we also resonate with the nature and strength of the universe—we awaken to a full realization of God.

Day 31
—◆—
Wings of Prayer

"Prayer is the soul's sincere desire."

—JAMES MONTGOMERY

The Butterfly

By Donna Miesbach

I've caught the sunlight in my wings
And move with ease and grace
For Spirit is my medium
And earth my dwelling place.
But once I crawled on tiny feet
Amid the dust of earth
Until at last I turned within
And found my own new birth.
'Tis through the chrysalis of prayer
My soul now freely sings
For when at last I did emerge,
Christ light was captured in my wings.
Yes, I am ever Spirit's child,
All grace and ease commanding,
Born within a moment
Of quiet understanding.

Dear God,

I may have encountered both high and low points in life, but most certainly the elevation of the mountaintop experiences would not have seemed so high without the deep experiences in the recesses of the valleys.

And when I am going through a valley of despair, I keep my eyes on the mountaintop. I do this by letting my prayers bring me higher to a greater realization of You. Aware of You, I actually feel sadness and depression lessen. The more I am aware of You, the fewer negative thoughts and feelings I have.

So if ever I think that I am being called upon to do more than I am capable of doing for my family, on the job, or for myself, I let my thoughts be lifted on the wings of prayer. I understand that Your spiritual power and wisdom are within me. And, God, I call upon You to *be* more and *do* more through me.

In this quiet time of prayer, I am lifted to a greater realization of the power and wisdom of God within me.

Some Journaling Ideas

—— ◆ ——

1. What do I consider some of my mountaintop experiences?
2. How do I envision God being more and doing more through me?

Day 32
---◆---
New Creation

"To see things in the seed,
that is genius."

—LAO-TZU

I Am Stronger
Than My Fears

By Hannah More Kohaus

I am stronger than my fears,
I am wiser than my years,
I am gladder than my tears;
    For I am God's image.

I am better than my deeds,
I am holier than my creeds,
I am wealthier than my needs;
    For I am God's image.

God, whose image thus I bear
And whose likeness I shall share,
All God's glory will declare
    Through the "I": God's image.

Dear God,

A glorious feeling of peace is rising from within my soul. Because I know I am eternally one with You, I no longer feel the urge to worry or fret. In some ways, I may still look the same as the person I was only weeks ago, but now my eyes reflect the peace in my soul. I give love from my heart that can be felt and experienced by all who know me.

God, You have given me the freedom to discover the wonder I am capable of being and accomplishing, and I thank You for this privilege. The peace I feel is only a minuscule portion of the abundance You offer me every day. Now that I have felt the serenity of Your presence so fully, I will keep that feeling with me forever. I have experienced a rebirth of my spiritual oneness with You, and I am a new creation! I lack nothing because You are all there is, all there will ever be.

Yes, God, I welcome and honor Your presence in my life, for You are the one true presence and power.

In this quiet time of prayer, I honor my spiritual oneness with God.

Some Journaling Ideas

———◆———

1. What positive results will likely occur from my acceptance of becoming a new person?
2. How do I honor God's presence in everyday living?

Day 33
— ◆ —
Living My Dream

"The human spirit cannot be paralyzed. If you are breathing, you can dream."

—MIKE BROWN

Listening with Soul

By Barbara Bergen

I am a part
       . . . a very small part . . .
              of an all-encompassing Whole.

I can tune in
    with my inner ear
       to intuitive messages soft, yet clear,
          When I listen with my soul.

Dear God,

I understand now that the greatest desires of my heart cannot be found in the physical world. Over a lifetime, I have set and achieved many goals, and I recognize them for what they are: stepping-stones that brought me to where I am today.

And now I know, God, that the only worthwhile dreams are the ones that lead me to a greater understanding of You—Your spirit within me and within all. The more I seek You, the more I feel Your presence and order in every area of my life.

As each day unfolds, Your light shines brighter *in* me. Your light shining *from* me reveals wonder all around me, and I experience the glory of Your loving presence.

Yes, God, I am living my dream because I am living Your light.

In this quiet time of prayer, the way to live my dreams is revealed.

Some Journaling Ideas

—— ◆ ——

1. What ideas come to mind that may be my greatest desires?
2. How can my dreams help me accomplish something meaningful?

*"Our Creator would never have
made such lovely days and
have given us the deep hearts to
enjoy them unless we were meant
to be immortal."*

—NATHANIEL HAWTHORNE

Communion

By Donna Miesbach

Smooth as glassy seas
My mind is in repose
Waiting for the message
That only Spirit knows,
Waiting for the channel
Deep within to be re-formed
As secret inner urgings
Strive to be re-born.
Silent are the workings
Of this mighty power
That speaks within the waiting soul
At this holy hour.

Dear God,

My quest to know more of the truth about myself is a day-to-day discovery of who I am and what I am capable of achieving.

Each day, I am learning more and more that the most powerful statement I can begin and end my day with is *"I Am!"* As I say these words in conjunction with whatever I do—the decisions I make, the actions I take—I am infusing my mental and physical abilities with spiritual power.

I am absolute love—You have shown me this, God—and I *am* worthy of being loved and loving. I accept the promise of Your life in me, knowing that I *am* created in Your likeness and I *am* capable of tremendous things.

From this day forward—in partnership with You—I am living a spiritually enriched life.

In this quiet time of prayer, I make a conscious connection with my spiritual identity.

Some Journaling Ideas

— ◆ —

1. What will I put on my list of things to do that "I am" statements will help me in doing and being?
2. How willing am I to use positive affirmations that enrich my confidence and my day?

Day 35
—◆—
Faith

*"Take the first step in faith.
You don't have to see the whole
staircase, just take the first step."*

—MARTIN LUTHER KING JR.

Blossom of Faith

By Elaine Meyer

A rose,
Unfolding,
Beautiful and perfect,
Greeting the morning sun,
Inspiring, breathtaking,
God's gift to me.

My faith,
Ever-growing,
Persistent and strong,
Seeing me through all things,
Ceaseless, unwavering,
My gift to God.

Dear God,

Sometimes, I feel that I can't make it through what lies ahead. Then I remember to look back on my life. As I go over the experiences that have led me to this moment, I understand more clearly that You were with me all along. It's You that I have faith in—unquestionably.

Through all the ups and downs, even when I was least aware of it, Your loving presence was with me to soothe and comfort, to help me and give me strength. Through eyes of faith, I see that Your presence was the inspiration for the loving support I received from family and friends, the grace within the events that changed my life forever.

Moment by moment, hour by hour, the experiences of my life have come together to form a strong foundation on which I build hope. Day by day, year after year, my faith in You grows, gaining in strength and giving me the confidence I need to get through even the toughest times.

In this quiet time of prayer,
my faith is strengthened.

Some Journaling Ideas

———— ◆ ————

1. What times stand out in my memory as moments of faith?
2. How does a current challenging situation look through the eyes of faith?

Day 36
◆
Pieces of the Puzzle

"You see things and say, 'Why?', but I dream things and say, 'Why not?'"

—GEORGE BERNARD SHAW

The Lighthouse

By Shirley Mozelle

It's true that light
is the source,
a lamp inside
that lights the soul,
but it is the eye itself,
a focused lens,
that bends and shapes
and makes the beam.

Dear God,

Although I may not understand why something is happening to me or to someone I love, I know that divine order—Your order—is guiding us. Because this is so, I don't feel it is necessary to always know the details of where some experience is leading me or what the end result will be. All I need to know is that You are in charge.

As I have faith in You, God, and as I take action on that faith, I begin to see that every experience is an important piece of the puzzle of my life. Each piece of that puzzle has shaped me into the person I now am—the whole that is *me*.

Acknowledging the importance of every event helps me release the hurts and fears that I may have been holding on to. As I let them go, I see the overall picture of my life that is emerging, and it is a life of beauty and wonder.

In this quiet time of prayer, I perceive that every event can be important in the whole scheme of my life.

Some Journaling Ideas

— ◆ —

1. What have I learned from yesterday's events?
2. How might past experiences help me today?

Day 37
—◆—
Momentum

"Shoot for the moon. Even if you miss, you will land among the stars."

—LES BROWN

Divine Balance

By Norman V. Olsson

May I always yield to the deep calm
    of the night, feel its healing balm;
Quick to surrender when it is time
    to rest in God's safe, peaceful clime.

Then, when morning dew, sunlight return,
    reborn, I face life with unconcern.
I have learned that day and night provide
    such balance found in ocean tide.

"For everything there is a season,"
    the prophet spoke with good reason.
Life's ebb and flow fare well for my soul;
    each changing phase helps me keep whole!

Dear God,

There may be times when I feel disappointed with myself—as if I am not making progress, as if I am moving in slow motion with no visible results of success.

Yet with every day of my life dedicated to knowing You, I can't help but become more aware of Your presence in everything I do. I do trust You, God, and know that my faith grows a day at a time. My faith in You will bring out the best in me.

As my faith picks up momentum, I see that the road ahead smooths out before me. And while there may still be bumps along the way, I understand that they are simply there to slow me down so that I can look around and enjoy the scenery of life.

Every day of my life I am making progress! And every day of my life I am building momentum. I am moving forward toward blessings I have never before imagined were possible!

In this quiet time of prayer, I feel the momentum of my faith building.

Some Journaling Ideas

———◆———

1. When am I most aware of God?
2. How do I determine if I am making progress in my spiritual unfoldment?

_____

_____

_____

_____

_____

_____

_____

_____

_____

_____

_____

_____

_____

_____

_____

_____

Day 38
—◆—
Work in Progress

*"Love yourself for every effort
you make . . . every good desire
you feel . . . every small bit of
courage you show."*

—MARY KUPFERLE

Mark of the Maker

By R. H. Grenville

God, as Creator, engineers
things delicate and grand:
rainbows, stars, and mountain peaks,
a newborn baby's hand;
the quasar's pulse, the rhythmic tides,
spheres and polygons;
the cheerfulness of chickadees,
the elegance of swans.

Nothing is simply "good enough"
that God has brought to be.
To each is given a special touch
of loving artistry:
each blade of grass, each grain of sand,
each leaf to bud or fall,
each person, place, and power and thing
a signed original.

Dear God,

I am amazed at the fantastic possibilities some days offer me. Thank You for the new doors that are opening to me! I enter through them with great anticipation, always knowing that as one door closes, another opens.

So even if I appear to have failed at something, I am not a failure. I have succeeded when I have done my best. And even seeming failures are useful, for I take whatever I have learned and apply it in my plans for today and for the future. I am a work in progress, and I grow more complete and stronger every day.

Like the caged bird that sings a song born of the freedom it feels in its soul, I, too, know a peace in my heart that can never be taken away—no matter the circumstances.

I continue making progress, for the peace and the joy of knowing You are always with me.

In this quiet time of prayer, I become aware of all the possibilities that are open to me.

Some Journaling Ideas

— ◆ —

1. What experiences have I labeled "negative" that I now understand are ones from which I have gained new strength and confidence?
2. Of all that I do, what do I feel most fulfilled in doing?

Day 39
—◆—
One Step

"I am not discouraged, because every wrong attempt discarded is another step forward."

—THOMAS A. EDISON

Inner Journey

By Barbara Bergen

Roads stretch far to the mountains.
Highways wind clear out of sight.
But the path I love best winds inward
To the heart of God's radiant light.

Though I travel the world about me,
Contentment doesn't begin
Till I choose the journey inward—
The path to my soul within.

Dear God,

Why is it that when I have the chance for greater happiness or achievement, I cannot always accept it? Only one step away from what seems to be a golden moment, something inside me cautions me *not* to move into it.

Even as I ask You why I hesitate, I feel the reassurance of Your trust in me. It's as if You are telling me that it's okay to pause, to take the next step with faith and purpose. From You, I understand that every step can be a time of achievement, a golden moment of its own. I don't rush into any situation, because I want You to guide me.

It is exciting to think I am one step away from a blessing, but, oh, what a celebration I feel knowing that each moment in life is a blessing from You! Each moment will be golden when I am aware of You.

In this quiet time of prayer, I step forward into a golden moment with God.

Some Journaling Ideas

—— ◆ ——

1. When have I felt most comfortable in making a decision?
2. What motivates me the most in my times of spiritual renewal?

"*The Father and I are one.*"

—JESUS

God Lives as Thee

By Jim Rosemergy

May you sleep in God's peace;
Wake in God's joy;
Walk in God's light;
And be warmed by God's love.
And all that you are and will ever be
Is all because God lives as thee.

Dear God,

I may have begun this prayer journal as a search for You, but You have gently and lovingly expanded my vision to take in the sacredness of all You have created.

God, I truly believe that I can never again feel alone, for You are my very life. No matter where I may be, I will be in Your presence. No matter whom I am with, I will recognize the majesty of Your creation.

In my search for my own spirituality, I have discovered that although the world in which I live is full of physical wonder and beauty, it is also *home* for all Your beloved. Every person, animal, and plant is unique and has a purpose to fulfill.

The unity I feel with all life is confirmation that I am aware of You not only as *my* God but also as the God of *all*. This is a wonderful life, God, and I live it in oneness with You and with all that You are.

In this quiet time of prayer, I experience a oneness with God that is a oneness with all life.

Some Journaling Ideas

———◆———

1. Can I name at least three positives I experienced in praying, journaling, and reading inspirational material each day?
2. What will prompt me in the days and years ahead to keep in touch with my sacred soul?

ABOUT THE
FEATURED AUTHORS

Section 1: Works of Art, Signed by God

Fannie Flagg is a successful actress, novelist, and screenwriter. Her books include the *New York Times* bestseller *Fried Green Tomatoes at the Whistle Stop Cafe, Daisy Fay and the Miracle Man*, and *Fannie Flagg's Original Whistle Stop Cafe Cookbook*.

She received the prestigious Scripters Award and was nominated for both the Writers Guild of America Award and an Academy Award for her screenplay for the movie *Fried Green Tomatoes*.

Section 2: Honoring Our Spirituality in Prayer

Jackie Nink Pflug was a passenger on EgyptAir Flight 648 on Thanksgiving weekend of 1985. She was traveling from Athens, Greece, back to her teaching assignment in Cairo, Egypt, when terrorists hijacked the plane.

Pflug was one of a few to survive the hijacking, but because of a serious gunshot injury to the head, she was left with physical challenges and memory loss. She captures the drama of her remarkable healing and spiritual awakening in her book, *Miles to Go before I Sleep*. Pflug is currently in demand as a motivational speaker.

Section 3: Surrendering to Love

Gerald G. Jampolsky, M.D., has gained international recognition for his work with children who have catastrophic illnesses. In 1975, he established the Center for

Attitudinal Healing. There are now more than 120 centers around the world in 18 countries.

Dr. Jampolsky is author of several books, including the bestseller *Love Is Letting Go of Fear*, and has appeared on such television programs as *60 Minutes*, *Today*, and *The Oprah Winfrey Show*.

Section 4: Awakening to God

Duke Tufty serves as minister at Unity Temple on the Plaza in Kansas City, Missouri. In addition, he is president of the Cornerstone Foundation, an organization that presents spirituality seminars featuring nationally known speakers.

ABOUT THE EDITORS

As with most individuals who make up a team, editors Colleen Zuck, Janie Wright, and Elaine Meyer share many common interests. Yet their different backgrounds and life experiences are a rich source of inspiration in writing *Daily Word* magazine messages in a language that is understood as much by the souls as by the minds of readers around the world.

Perhaps one thing they have most in common—among themselves, with their *Daily Word* co-workers, Linda Kahler and Jill Delfenthal, and with all others who serve with them in the Silent Unity Prayer Ministry—is a commitment to merge with the one voice that is Silent Unity, a voice that shares a message of love and prayer support with all who are willing to hear.

Dear Friend . . .

For forty days, you've committed yourself to spiritual growth. Perhaps you read this book because the title gave you hope for the spiritual awakening you longed for. Now that you have finished it—become aware that something very powerful has taken place within you and is *continuing* to take place—you have experienced an awakening of the sacred soul, a reawakening to your own spirituality.

As you continue to commit yourself and your life to the soul-awakening experiences of the past forty days, you will find that they have become the new focus, the new commitment of your life. Far from an ending, you will come to know that completing this book is a beginning for you. Just as surely as you need to be consciously awake each day you also need to be spiritually awake.

And for thousands of people around the world, there is a prayer that has served as a wake-up call to the sacred soul. From one voice to another, the "Prayer for Protection" has circled Earth, but the truth contained in this powerful little poem could not be contained by Earth's atmosphere. A copy of this prayer was launched into outer space with astronaut Edwin E. "Buzz" Aldrin and even accompanied him on his historic moon walk. So wherever you may go—as far away as outer space or into the inner space of your sacred soul—let the message of God's presence accompany you.

May the awakening of your soul be your commitment forever. And may your life be enriched by the inner wisdom and power being expressed by you every day!

The *Daily Word* Staff

Prayer for Protection

By James Dillet Freeman

The light of God surrounds me;
The love of God enfolds me;
The power of God protects me;
The presence of God watches over me.
Wherever I am, God is!

An Invitation

Daily Word is the magazine of Silent Unity, a worldwide prayer ministry now in its second century of service. Silent Unity believes that:

- *All people are sacred*
- *God is present in all situations*
- *Everyone is worthy of love, peace, health, and prosperity*

Silent Unity prays with all those who ask for prayer. Every prayer request is held in absolute confidence, and there is never a charge. You are invited to contact Silent Unity 24 hours a day, any day of the year.

Write: Silent Unity
            1901 NW Blue Parkway
            Unity Village, MO 64065-0001

Or call: (816) 969-2000
Fax: (816) 251-3554
Online: http://www.dailyword.org

There's More!

If you enjoy these inspirational messages, you may wish to subscribe to *Daily Word* magazine and receive a fresh, contemporary, uplifting message for each day of the month. With its inclusive, universal language, this pocket-size magazine is a friend to millions of people around the world. For subscription information or to receive a free sample copy of *Daily Word* in English (regular and large-type editions) or in Spanish, please write to the above address.

Or call: (800) 669-0282

INDEX OF POETRY